FASHION PUBLICATION:
EXPOSING MEANING IN FASHION THROUGH PRESENTATION
EDITED BY PATRICK LI PUBLISHED BY CREATIVE TIME, INC.
CONCEIVED WITH ANDREA ROSEN/AGENCY FOR EXCEPTIONAL PROJECTS©

COMFORTABLE

OFF BALANCE
SERENITY

BRIGHT
PEACE

NO
SOUND

COMME des GARÇONS
*

"SCENES FROM COMME DES GARÇONS' NEW FLAGSHIP STORE IN AOYAMA, TOKYO, PHOTOS MASAYUKI HAYASHI"

GUCCI

DKNY

JIL SANDER

CREATIVE TIME IN THE ANCHORAGE: EXPOSING MEANING IN FASHION THROUGH PRESENTATION

Exhibition May 19 - July 18, 1999

1   Installations by Hussein Chalayan, Susan Cianciolo, Maison Martin Margiela, Viktor & Rolf and Vivienne Westwood

2   Fashion Publication re-presenting fashion photography edited by Patrick Li.

3   Loud & Unhinged, a media environment by Victoria Bartlett and Richard Pandiscio with Douglas Keeve, Mark Robbin, and Big Room

4   Four nights of music in June organized by Keving McHugh

note   This project was conceived with Andrea Rosen/Agency for Exceptional Projects©

For more than twenty-five years, Creative Time has commissioned adventurous public works of art by artists of all disciplines. Our history has been defined by our risk-taking spirit and our commitment to artistic excellence. We have boldly introduced audiences to challenging ideas about cultural practice and invigorated public spaces with cutting-edge works by visual artists as well as media makers, performers, musicians, architects, poets, and graphic designers. Yet despite our respect for all art forms, Creative Time has rarely worked with fashion designers—a surprising omission considering fashion design can be a powerful and creative means of artistic expression. In response to this situation, Creative Time was eager to create serious programs that both illuminate the depth of creativity in fashion design and honor it as an important artistic endeavor. We sought the advice of many people in the fashion and art communities—the most important of whom was Andrea Rosen/Agency for Exceptional Projects©. From our conversations emerged Creative Time's fashion initiative. Our initial project, the Exquisite Corpse Series, took place in the Fall of 1997 in the windows of Saks Fifth Avenue and marked our first significant effort in working with fashion designers. Realizing there was a pressing curatorial need to expose artistic integrity in fashion design, we decided to create a new project that would examine the particular potency of fashion through its various modes of presentation. The result is Creative Time in the Anchorage: Exposing Meaning in Fashion Through Presentation. This multi-faceted project features this publication as well as installations, a media environment, and a music series all taking place at the landmark Brooklyn Bridge Anchorage. In conceiving this project, Andrea Rosen poignantly argued that if we were to ask designers to create works for the Anchorage, the context had to be compatible to their vision and practice. She selected designers, who share a strong commitment to their artistry, and to the investigation into the creative and intellectual possibilities of presentation, to create installations in the Anchorage. We are proud that Hussein Chalayan, Susan Cianciolo, Maison Martin Margiela, Viktor & Rolf, and Vivienne Westwood accepted our invitation to transform the cathedralesque chambers of the Anchorage with site-specific installations. We are deeply grateful to them for recognizing the importance of this initiative and committing their time to making this effort a reality. With these designers in place, we looked to our highly creative and energetic colleagues, Victoria Bartlett and Richard Pandiscio, to create a complementary installation that would explore the relationship between media and fashion presentation. They in turn partnered with Douglas Keeve, Mark Robbin and Big Room to create "Loud and Unhinged," an immersive media environment exploring the link between film, art, and fashion. To strengthen this investigation, we turned to our respected friend, Patrick Li, to realize a project which would recognize exceptional fashion presentation in print. Rather than creating an exhibition of fashion photography at the Anchorage, we chose to package this project in the form of a magazine. This publication features some of the most inspired fashion photography recently published in various international magazines. It also features publication-specific contributions and selections of compelling ad campaigns by some of today's most remarkable fashion designers. Creative Time in the Anchorage: Exposing Meaning in Fashion Through Presentation could not have happened without the friendship of many people, all of whom have worked passionately to make our dream a reality. I am joined by Creative Time's Board and staff in expressing that it has been an honor and privilege to work with the participating designers and curators, as well as the artists, photographers, magazines, and filmmakers who have so generously shared their vision. Finally, we are deeply grateful to our sponsors who believe in Creative Time and the value of this initiative. In particular, for this publication, we are most indebted to Mead for its generous gift of Signature® paper and to Print International for going the extra mile to make this publication the stunning product it is. Anne Pasternak, Executive Director, Creative Time

The other day a reporter called me to discuss the project, Exposing Meaning in Fashion Through Presentation. He wanted to know why visual arts organizations and the art world were so fascinated with fashion. My first response was "what does this project have to do with art and why do you consider Creative Time to be a visual arts organization?" Creative Time is an organization specifically set up to expose various creative endeavors in contexts particularly appropriate to those endeavors. His question represents the heart of a dilemma within the rubric of artistic activity and my reasoning for conceiving this project. Why can we see music, performing arts, and film as viable creative practices separate and equal to visual art, yet the value of fashion is always questioned? Why do people (including people in the fashion community) assume that the easiest way to legitimize fashion as a meaningful artistic discipline is by creating a link with visual art? Although it does not appear in our press release, two of the three press previews published to date in leading magazines took it upon themselves to promote the project as "the merger of art and fashion" or "art installations." Why is it perceived that fashion isn't enough on its own? I think, ultimately it's a problem of understanding that meaning comes in many different forms. There is a laziness that assumes that we need an isolated experience, i.e. going to a museum, concert, or performance, to know that we have had a significant or altering encounter. This begins to explain why the discipline of fashion as an art form might be questioned at first. But why the constant linking of visual art and fashion? I can only imagine that this must have something to do with opposites attracting. Art is all about permanency and fashion is all about the moment. I think Western culture is obsessed with the immortal gesture—something that will last forever and ever, or something that will be reinterpreted for thousands of years to come. Typically, creating this immortal gesture is the challenge visual artists must face in order to be legitimized. Great artists are only great when proven by history. Our obsession with heroic immortality—basically our fear of death—seems to discourage us from believing that there is significance in the momentary and the fleeting. It almost comes down to metaphysics. I would think that most people believe in the reality of permanency. What you see and feel and hear is real, that which can physically move through time. We therefore generally tend to undervalue the unseen, the less perceivable day to day influence that constantly changes the fabric of universal thinking and action. Where art is easily honorable because of its emphasis on permanency, fashion's core meaning lies in its transient nature. Perhaps our fear of the less tangible makes it easy, if not desirable, to ignore the optimism that is imbedded in the momentary. Fashion, in its constant flux, embodies the hope that change, although not always equal to progress, can transform into inspiration and even evolution. Perhaps the art world's fascination with fashion is a recognition of fashion's ability to address every day influence instead of the obsession with the heroics of creating history. I am not interested in "interdiscipline envy." What I am interested in is defining, equalizing, and strengthening the roles of each creative process. In the particular case of this project, I hope to expose meaning within fashion. Not to compare and contrast or intertwine fashion with art but, to present fashion as fashion. There is no presumption that we have represented fashion fully or in its myriad of forms. There are no clothes displayed and no runway shows. In order to emphasize specificity of intent, or to expose where and how clarity already does exist within fashion, we have chosen to present three modes of presentation: installation, print, and film/video. In the development of each of the three arenas there was the same questioning: "when and how are these mediums best used to emphasize content and when is the medium used purposefully to maximize impact?" Our criteria was not to pick our favorite designers and ask them to do installations. We chose designers for whom physical presentation/installation has always been at the core of their work. We did not choose to simply survey the magazines we might think are important or interesting. We chose to present a curated project that we felt emphasized when editors, stylists, photographers, and advertisers clearly acknowledge the particular impact of the print medium. In keeping with our focus we were not interested in decontextualizing the images, hence our choice to publish this curated project in it's intrinsic form, a magazine. In addressing the role of film and video and it's relationship to exposing meaning in fashion, we did not chose to follow the example of other venues in which designers were arbitrarily requested to present their work in the form of film. Films/videos have been chosen to emphasis how film has influenced fashion and how fashion has influenced film. I hopefully by exposing clarity of intent we can encourage clarity of intent as well as illuminate the optimistic potency of fashion. Andrea Rosen for The Agency For Exceptional Projects ©

I am a magazine junkie. During my early college years, I sold magazines from around the world at Dave's Smokeshop in Berkeley. Among my responsibilities, which included picking candy of the week, I selected magazines to be displayed in the store window. Every week I went through the new arrivals to determine if they were worthy of distinction. The decision to highlight selected magazines was based on finding something unexpected: an interesting article or amazing images. Those with any value transcended the fleeting moment, and somewhere between then and now, I realized that magazines were only as good as their content. Invited by Creative Time to curate a component of Exposing Meaning in Fashion Through Presentation, I was challenged to select images that illuminate outstanding fashion presentation in print. Although broad in scope, the concept of presentation in fashion images is rather definite. Presentable images show clarity of intent and excellence through the execution of a specific concept. The images define the concept and the concept is manifested in the images. The concept often benefits from a stylist's choice of clothes or an art director's layout or graphic treatment. This inextricable layer adds to images that stand firm for a moment, however fleeting, against the tide of fashionable change. By presenting the unexpected, outstanding presentations in print challenge the inevitable moment of obsolescence the very instant they are experienced. Fashion, in its many modes of presentation, stops for no one, no style, no single idea, but these images force the viewer to take a second look. Speaking to Anne Pasternak and Andrea Rosen regarding how to most appropriately exhibit fashion in print within the framework of the project, it became clear that printing a publication would be ideal. By re-presenting selected images in the form of a magazine, we would maintain the integrity of their original form. The images appear as they did within their original publications; indeed, most pages are reproduced from tearsheets. Holding the object, turning the pages and revisiting previously seen images is in itself the message and the experience. Editorial images are only one aspect of published fashion presentation. Recognizing that designers also direct their own presentation in print, we wanted to create space to honor their vision. We therefore invited those designers in the exhibition as well as select others to create specially-designed contributions for this publication. Finally, in an effort to both distinguish those designers who are committed to expressing their unique vision through creative advertising and to reinforce the context of a magazine, we featured specific campaigns. The images on the following pages have been selected from the past six or seven seasons. The time period is broad enough to present a variety of images while allowing for an investigation within a recent visual history. Editing thousands of pages from hundreds of magazines down to our 160 pages does not allow for complete stories; instead, each spread intends to pose questions of selection. Fashion Publication is not meant to be an anthology of the best fashion photography from this period. Many more stories were originally chosen than could be represented here. Their exclusion by no means negates their importance as they all contribute to a larger sense of place and awareness that inform selection and choice. My thanks are extended to all of the designers, photographers and magazines, and many others that have participated in this selection of outstanding fashion presentation in print. Patrick Li

Fashion, film, and art mirror one another—bouncing and rebounding, mixing, and swirling in a lather of give and take. For Creative Time, we've selected examples of fashion-concerned presentations, as seen on film and video, which we think point towards new and meaningful ways fashion may be cast in the future—to entertain, reflect, and sell the stories fashion will always tell us about who we are. Victoria Bartlett and Richard Pandiscio

MAGAZINE MAY/JUNE 1999

KAHIMI KARIE

DENNIS HOPPER

RUTH ROGERS

WAYNE
KOESTENBAUM

RICHARD
FOREMAN

DESIGNER'S STATEMENTS:

Presentation is a frame for ideas.   Hussein Chalayan

It should be noted, in regard to the work of Susan Cianciolo that the presentation of a given collection is in no way separate from the total concept. That is to say, that collections are conceived as an entire cohesive unit, with each element giving power to the other in order to create a whole. The stitch is important to the garment as the garment is important to the exhibition as the exhibition is important to the stitch. There is no separation, mentally or physically. This approach allows the designer to break free from the constraints of the market (models, runways, glamour, hoopla) and at the same time, be it intentionally or not, re-configure the code that created them. It is important to note, however, that the rejection of the standard runway show is not the result of a rebellion against the traditional norms of fashion presentation. It is rather a natural extension of the ideas of the collection, if a runway show were to fit the concept it would be employed. The concepts of Run Collection are anti-marketing, anti-hype, and pro-creation. Any similarities to the outside are purely coincidental. There are no rules in this game, except that the decisions be natural, without regard to trends, conventions, or industry standards. Run Collection has spawned from a generation of creators who are not so willing to be defined by the labels of the past. All creative options are open, and there to be taken advantage of. Cinema, installation, performance, publishing, are now readily accessible and therefore applied to make manifest a concept. Presentations are the result of pure, untainted vision, without influence from outside sources or traditions unless they happen to occur naturally. The limits of what a designer can and cannot do are dissolving and legions of Run Collection imitations are testament to this fact. The industry is changing and it has nothing to do with what has happened before. The leaders of yesterday must now become followers or accept to be left in the dust.   Aaron Rose for Susan Cianciolo/Run Collection

Fashion can be artistic. It's a question of the manipulation of materials and how much control you have over those. Once you master a technique, self expression can happen, so it's artistic and let's just say that about fashion. Art and fashion is a problematic mix. Art is an elitist activity, not fashion.   Vivienne Westwood

Caught by the gaze of the audience as animals in headlights, fashion designers appear from behind their work only in passing: in the very moment of the shock of the new, the flash of the camera, the blink of the critic's eye. The dialectical moment of seeing-and-being-seen is in fashion's grip. Imprisonment in the visibility of fashion may appear a voluntary one, but from both sides of the glimmering, blinding bars, there is no escape from visuality. We are captured within this spectacle this is haunted by the emptiness it is trying to veil.   Our work is a commentary on the status of couture as a folding and unfolding of a void. Couture is not a craft but rather an era, the promise of which has been forgotten. Couture should be a laboratory of experiments resulting not in final products, but in ideas in the process of being formed. We consider ourselves not the agents, but the authors of our vision, looking from inside out, and from outside in, as our work emerges from this intersection.   Viktor & Rolf

Maison Martin Margiela.
2, bis Passage Ruelle,
75018 Paris.

Fax to :   Creative Time, New York
               Anne Pasternak, Wendy Dembo & Patrick Li.

From: Maison Martin Margiela, Paris.
               Patrick Scallon.

RE: **Maison Martin Margiela Exhibition (9/4/1615)**

NL 1997:	The Museum Boijmans van Beuningen, Rotterdam.	June 11th 1997 to August 17th 1997
JAPAN 1999:	The National Museum of Art, Kyoto	April 6th 1999 to August 4th 1999
JAPAN 1999:	The National Museum of Art, Tokyo	August 6th 1999 to September 6th 1999
USA 1999:	Creative Time, The Brooklyn Anchorage, New York.	May 19th 1999 to July 18th 1999

[ABRIDGED VERSION OF THE ORIGINAL STATEMENT ISSUED IN 1997: COMMENCES]

Over the past ten months Maison Martin Margiela has been working on the first Martin Margiela solo exhibition, entitled **(9/4/1615)**.

The Museum Boijmans van Beuningen invited Maison Martin Margiela to mount an exhibition of its work to be held in their 'glass pavilion'. Martin Margiela (9/4/1615) is the last exhibition to be held in the glass pavilion before its transformation later this year.

Maison Martin Margiela has produced a retrospective of its work (P/E 1989 - A/H 1997/8, 18 collections). Each collection is represented by one silhouette comprising garments that have been specially reproduced in whites, creams and greys.

We proposed that the exhibition be in collaboration with a prominent Dutch Microbiologist, Dr A.W.S.M van Egeraat, Professor at the Wareningen Agricultural University, The Netherlands. Dr Van Egeraat's specialisation has been on Pea-root exudates and their effect upon root-nodule bacteria.

Each outfit has been treated with varying types of bacteria , yeast and mould isolated from the air and nurtured to provide varying colours and textures. Over the first five days of the exhibition these organisms developed on the clothes and, once their gestation period was complete, changed the colour and aspect of the garments.

All of the eighteen silhouettes remain on the exterior of the pavilion and may only be viewed from the inside through its glass structure. The catalogue of the exhibition is more a handbook to assist those viewing the eighteen dressed mannequins. Its structure comprises three books. ISBN Number 90-6918-180-0.

[ABRIDGED VERSION OF ORIGINAL STATEMENT ISSUED IN 1997: ENDS]

[Q&A ORIGINALLY ANSWERED FOR OPENING IN 1997: COMMENCES]

WHY DID YOU CHOOSE TO WORK WITH A MICROBIOLOGIST FOR YOUR FIRST SOLO EXHIBITION - (9/4/1615)
June 11 - August 17th 1997, Rotterdam, The Netherlands ?

The Museum Boijmans van Beuningen approached us with their proposition of an exhibition. They requested that, if we were to mount an exhibition, it should be in their glass pavilion and figure in a series of collaborative exhibitions that they have had in the pavilion. Our exhibition was to be the last held in the pavilion prior to its closure and returbishment as the restaurant of the Museum.

We were, in fact, little conscious or sensitive to (9/4/1615) being our first 'solo' exhibition. We have taken part in so many exhibitions at Museums and other spaces over the past nine years that we view our participation in any of them, group or solo, as an expression of our work. We invest the same work, time and 'expression' in any of them.

Our decision to collaborate with the microbiologist Dr A.W.S.M Van Egeraat, professor at the Wageningen Agricultural University in the Netherlands arose from our wish to collaborate with a domain other than the architectural field proposed by the museum and one not connected to our daily work.

We opted to have the 18 dressed mannequins of the exhibition on the exterior of the space so that they could only be viewed from the inside of the pavilion through its glass structure. The pavilion was left completely empty respecting its own form, it was the last occassion it could be seen in the way its architecht intended.

WHY BACTERIA ?

We only know that our choice of working with bacteria was a natural one for us, something that came about spontaneously. We leave the interpretation of our use of bacteria on our work up to those witnessing the union. If beauty is in the eye of the beholder so too, for us, is any interpretation of a project such as this. What people think is their own business.

What was fascinating was the reaction our decision of working with bacteria engendered in others throughout the entire development of the project. Many people, we have discovered, are fearful of the very idea of bacteria, yet, we are surrounded and covered by bacteria every waking and sleeping moment. People can be as afraid of the bacteria and moulds used in this exhibition, which were isolated from the air, as they can be afraid of a cheese sandwich.

Anders Edström

○ You will be fortunate in everything you put your hands to. ○

Video images © Maison Martin Margiela A/W 1999 - 2000

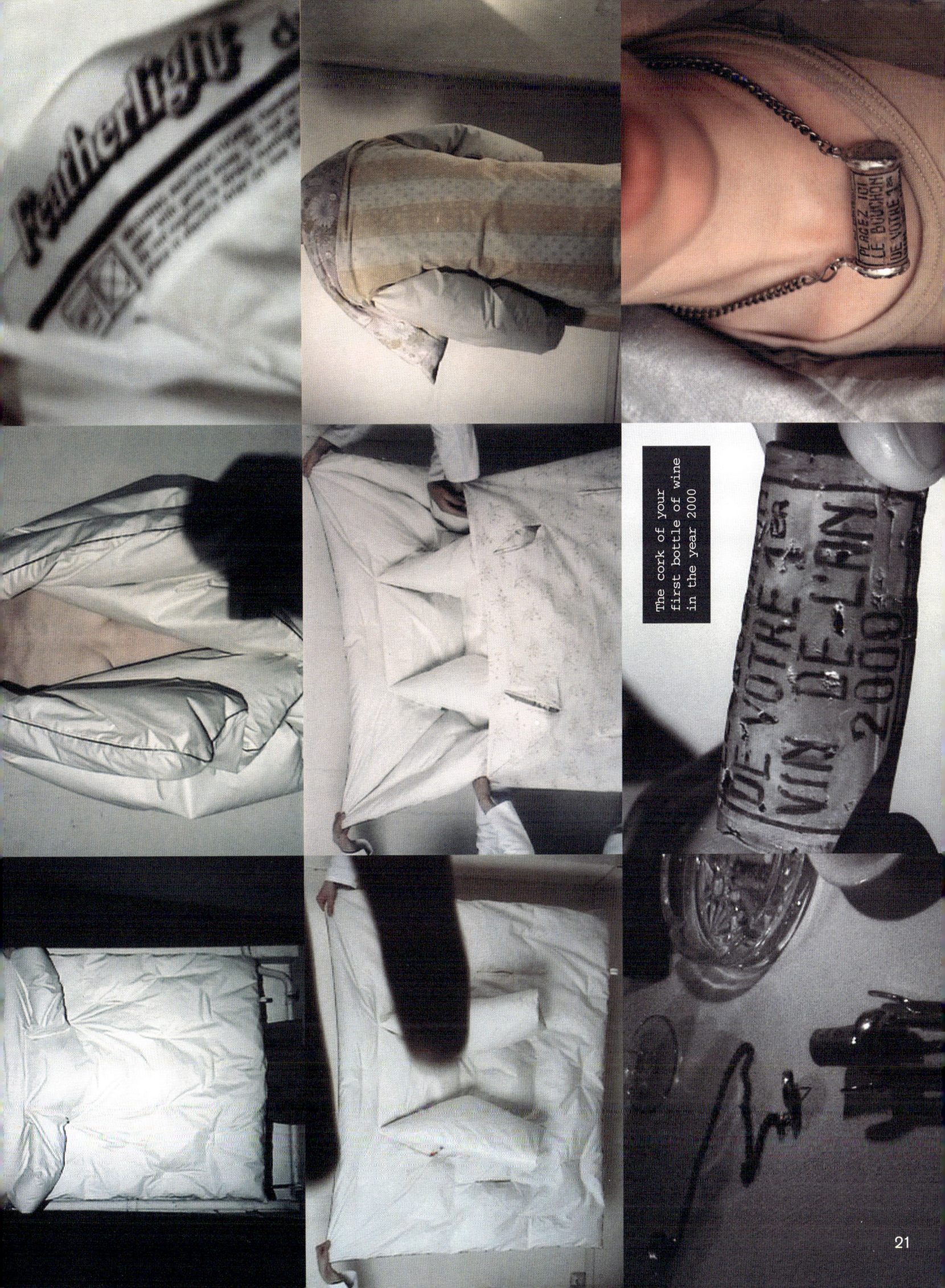

The cork of your
first bottle of wine
in the year 2000

21

IN THE NEWS SECTION

The cloning of the panda
HOME NEWS, PAGE 3

IN THE BROADSHEET REVIEW

Jeans: the Jeremy Clarkson effect
WEDNESDAY REVIEW FRONT

Suzanne Moore on Anna Ford
COMMENT, PLUS ARTS, FASHION &FINANCE

3,000 schools threatened with closure

By JUDITH JUDD
Education Editor

TEN PER CENT of all schools will be placed in a new category of poor schools and given a dead line of a year to improve, ministers said yesterday.

At present, 600 schools have been deemed to be failing by school inspectors and face closure unless they turn themselves around within two years.

A further 2,400 – around 10 per cent of all schools in England and Wales – have been found by inspectors to have serious weaknesses.

Stephen Byers, the school standards minister, said yesterday that the latter must turn themselves around within a year or they would be declared failing. He announced new measures to require local authorities to support schools with serious weaknesses and help them to draw up action plans with targets.

Ministers believe that early intervention is vital to prevent schools falling. Twenty-four local authorities keys that they should stay in after only six months if they believe a school is failing to make progress.

Under legislation before Parliament, councils will be able to appoint extra governors and withdraw the school's power to run its own budget.

At schools in the new category will be revisited by inspectors. Those with the worst reports will receive visits from inspectors from the Office for Standards in Education who will ask targets those in need and set a three-year truck record in helping struggling schools.

Any school found to have serious weaknesses will be monitored by Her Majesty's Inspector perhaps once or twice a year. All schools placed in the new category will face a further full inspection after two years.

Mr Byers said: "Today we recognise a new category of school – those with serious weaknesses. Our proposed action will ensure that there is early intervention to prevent seriously weak schools drifting into failure. Local education authorities must provide their schools with the support and guidance to turn themselves around.

"As we expect failing schools to be restored to health within two years, it should be possible for schools with serious weaknesses to do so within a much shorter period."

He said that the previous regime had treated all schools in the same way. Schools that were performing well should be given more freedom and the Government was already considering "lighter touch" inspections for them, he said.

David Hart, general secretary of the National Association of Head Teachers, backed the need to take action over poor schools but opposed the imposition of an artificial deadline.

"The circumstances surrounding schools with serious weaknesses are infinitely variable and the length of time it takes to get out of that category must inevitably vary."

Doug McAvoy, general secretary of the National Union of Teachers, said: "Schools with serious weaknesses have these weaknesses only in some aspects of their provision and they run alongside some excellent performance. If a school has the threat of possible closure hanging over it, it is in danger of losing those excellent teachers and that will make it even more difficult for it to turn around."

Schools may be declared to have serious weaknesses for a number of reasons: poor national test or exam results, a weak head, pupils who are making slow progress in the basics and unsatisfactory teaching in a quarter or more of lessons.

The new rules may help the Government to deal with a category of schools which have been causing increasing concern. An Audit Commission report earlier this year highlighted schools in only subject – those that looked good on the surface but were not doing enough for their children.

Because their middle class intake appeared other "they achieved reasonable exam results."

The Government is taking new powers to close failing schools which do not improve and to require them under poor management. As many as 15 schools failed by inspectors may close in September because they have failed to meet the new two-year deadline.

Ministers have abandoned the policy of "naming and shaming" failing schools after criticism from teacher unions and some headteachers who have succeeded in turning round poor schools.

Home Office says police patrols don't catch crooks

BY IAN BURRELL
Home Affairs Correspondent

MANY OF the high-profile crime-fighting initiatives of recent years have been a failure, according to Home Office research released yesterday. The controversial study concluded with a series of announcements by the Home Secretary, including a new £200m Crime Reduction Strategy.

Jack Straw said the new programme would only channel funds into schemes which had been shown to have a measurable impact on rates of crime.

In its detailed research the Home Office examined the value of past crime reduction projects, including populist schemes such as Neighbourhood Watch and extra "bobbies on the beat". It found that such measures can be "ineffective".

Instead, Mr Straw's new programme of initiatives will spend money on targeting and stopping repeat offenders.

Announcing the results of the Home Office Comprehensive Spending Review to Parliament, Mr Straw said the police would be given an extra £1.2bn over three years. A further £250m will be spent on expanding prison capacity in the same period and the Probation Service will get an extra £275m, enabling it to carry out new responsibilities like enhanced supervision of sex offenders.

In total, the Home Office budget is being extended by over three years.

The strategy will be overseen by a ministerial group bringing together the Home Secretary, the Attorney General, the Lord Chancellor and the Chief Secretary to the Treasury. Mr Straw said the group and its £250m budget represented "the largest commitment of its kind ever made in the world".

He said: "For many years governments concentrated too much on the consequences of crime to the detriment of its causes. But we can only make a long-term impact on crime and disorder by concentrating on both."

The new strategy was based largely on the findings of a three-year Home Office research project. It highlighted the ineffectiveness of numerous city-policing, where officers attempt to build better relations with the public to improve the flow of information about crime.

Neighbourhood Watch was found to flourish only in low-crime areas. The Home Office concluded that it was unlikely that the schemes "have had a marked effect in preventing crime nationally".

Nanny charged with murdering baby girl

By GLENDA COOPER
Social Affairs Correspondent

AN AUSTRALIAN nanny will stand trial at the Old Bailey after being charged with the murder of the baby Caroline Jespers. Louise Sullivan had previously been charged with causing grievous bodily harm to the child at the Jespers family home in north London earlier this year.

When the 26-year-old from Sydney appeared before Clerkenwell magistrates in north London yesterday that charge was dropped and replaced by one of murder. The case was committed for trial at the Old Bailey later this month.

Harlequins 'haute couture' from the autumn/winter 1998/99 collection by the Dutch designers Viktor and Rolf, showing in Paris yesterday   Peter Macdiarmid

Bailey at a date to be decided. Conditional bail was renewed, but with the additional requirement that Ms Sullivan does not seek employment caring for children, aged 16 or under while waiting for her trial.

At an inquest in London on 21 April, a pathologist, Dr Freddy Patel, testified that Caroline was probably a victim of "shaken baby syndrome". The baby was admitted to hospital on 11 April and died five days later when her life-support machine was switched off.

The case follows those of Louise Woodward, found guilty last year of the manslaughter of Matthew Eappen while working as an au pair, and of Helen Stacey who was jailed for life on Monday after being found guilty of shaking Joseph Mackie to death on 15 May last year.

Gawd 'elp us! Alf Garnett is resurrected

By PAUL McCANN

AFTER 7 YEARS of resting he was the nastiest, basest racist on television, Alf Garnett, the king of the curmudgeons, is to make his long-awaited return to the small screen with a one-off special for the BBC.

this autumn after six years in retirement.

ITV is to air a six-part series called The Thoughts of Chairman Alf in September, the last work of the scriptwriter Johnny Speight, the creator of Till Death Us Do Part who died earlier this month. The series is a

comp for ITV which has taken the character from the BBC.

The BBC aired the original sitcom to audiences of over 16 million when it was broadcast from 1965 to 1975. The BBC resurrected Alf broadcasting In Sickness and In Health from 1985 to 1992. The Thoughts of Chairman Alf take the form of a monologues in front of a theatre

audience as if the splenetic Alf was or a lecture later. Garnett, played as ever by Warren Mitchell, gives his views on all the old topics, such as the monarchy and immigration. Newfoundlanders will particularly enjoy his conservationist and rational rights.

The series was filmed six months ago and was inspired by a tour of Australia by the actor

Mitchell in 1995.

ITV had the idea of renewing the format when An Audience With ... starring Warren Mitchell and part-written by Speight, attracted a big audience last year.

"Alf Garnett is the most important comic character in British television history," said an ITV spokesman. "He was

an absolute legend, it would have been sacrilegious not to use the programme."

Speight died of cancer at the beginning of this month at the age of 78. When his comic creation appeared on screen in the Sixties it was the first time issues of politics, race and sex had been aired for a mass audience.

INSIDE

HOME NEWS

A mentally ill patient murdered his wife in 24 hours after being sent home from hospital.
PAGE 4

HOME NEWS

A bank force says urban bars should be allowed to serve drinks all day and all night.
PAGE 5

FOREIGN NEWS

P W Botha ordered the bombing of a church HQ while South Africa's president, it was claimed.
PAGE 13

BUSINESS

The chief executive of Life futures and pensions exchange in London has resigned.
PAGE 15

SPORT

Jacques Villeneuve, the F1 world champion, is quitting Williams to drive in the US
PAGE 26

Style

Floating on Millennium Optimism

From Visionaire's current Fantasy issue, Terry Richardson's clown-like interpretation of Valentino's party coat.

Fashion Sets The Tone for Celebration

By Suzy Menkes
International Herald Tribune

PARIS — Like a dedicated party-goer laying down champagne for future celebrations, fashion already seems to be in a pre-millennium mode. There is a mood of light-hearted optimism in clothes both in the street and on the catwalk — even before this year's end has been ritually feted on Thursday.

In contrast to the black, grungy, angst-ridden images that have dominated the 1990s, the predominant message from avant-garde designers is a feeling of hope and regeneration that traditionally comes with a new century.

Think of 1999 as the year of the balloon. The attempt last week by Richard Branson to float around the globe may have been a noble failure, but it captured the current madcap spirit.

Hey, you can't wear a balloon? Oh, yes you can! The inflatable dress is the ultimate in fashion whimsy for the new season.

First there were the swelling torsos, shoulders or necklines from the Dutch designers Viktor and Rolf, who filled out their colorful clothes with blown-up balloons inside them. Out bounced the outfit onto the runway — a Pierrot collar puffed up on a silver body suit or

a harlequin outfit with its bodice inflated like a life jacket. When the pneumatic effects were deflated, the extra folds of fabric just draped gracefully.

The witty and whimsical show of Yohji Yamamoto also had a blown-up dress — part of a bridal theme that had started the previous season with a wedding dress unfurled from strings like a parachute.

Then there are balloons as playful accessories. At the finale of Alberta Ferretti's spring-summer show in Milan, the models buried balloons around

as though they were chasing soap bubbles.

In a similar fashion spirit are puffball tulle skirts, voluminous but feather-light, from designers as diverse as the American Betsey Johnson, who even sent out a frilly tutu, to France's Thierry Mugler, whose models had dresses like spun sugar and hair in giant pompons.

If you were searching for a fun accessory for New Year's Eve, think of party favors to go with that sober little black dress. Colored streamers tied

Above, Thierry Mugler's tulle dress and puffball hair.

Far left, Viktor and Rolf's harlequin suit with blown-up bodice; left, their silver suit with inflated Pierrot collar.

Above right, Prada's jester cap and silk top with harlequin trim; above, Betsey Johnson's tulle-skirted Christmas fairy dress.

round the wrists at Christian Lacroix played on a ribbon theme that ran through the spring collections. There were ribbons decorating hems, weaving a lattice across a bodice, dangling at elbows from Marc Jacobs's pedal pushers or tied in bows down the spine of a good little girl's party dress from Ferretti.

What else is in the party spirit? The color ruffles at the shoulders (Lacroix), blouse hem (Gucci) or cascading down skirts (Alexander McQueen); balloon sleeves on peasant

Left, Lacroix's soft-shoulder dress and scarf stripjeans; above Jeremy Scott's gilded bow corset.

It symbolizes optimism to us — a time for celebration and that we have come out of a dark period of fashion and fashion images," said Cecilia Dean, one of the three founding editors, when she chose for a recent issue of Visionaire a Mario Sorrenti photograph in which the clothes were shown on figurines twisted from swankin's you knot in balloons.

The idea of fashion filling up with optimism and hope may be partly a switch of fashion's wheel, in which a smiling model becomes the shock of the new.

It could also be a response to public enmity against dull colors and minimalist design. Although grey has been the overwhelming fashion story for the winter season, a lot of that foggy flannel and olive cashmere has ended up in sale. Color is now the hot story, with red, sky blue, peppermint green and yellow coming to the fore and patterned fabrics making a comeback.

If fashion history is anything to go by,

the start of a century is often a time for lightening up. A new style blew in during the teens, matures in the '20s, solidifies in the middle years, rigidified by the '70s and is finally challenged by the century's end.

Things certainly went that way at the end of the 18th century, when the French Revolution and all its ferment luxury morphed into wispy, sheer empire dresses and the muslins of the Jane Austen era. Then came the nifty Victorian years with solid silhouettes and ponderous colors, before the lightening process began again under the Edwardians. Cropped hair and short skirts marked the early years of the 20th century.

So, at a playful mood, with a jester's hat, a stiff collar and folded bows, fashion prepares to slough off the fuzz tailoring and workmanlike separates that have marked the 20th century — and to green the coming millennium with a smile on the face and a bounce in the step.

BOOKS

MY GERMAN QUESTION
Growing Up in Nazi Berlin

By Peter Gay. 208 pages. $22.50. Yale.

Reviewed by Jonathan Yardley

PETER GAY, now emeritus professor of history at Yale, is well known in the scholarly and literary communities as the writer of numerous large and ambitious books, many dealing with social history and bourgeois life, nearly all heavily influenced by Freud. What is far less widely known is that although Gay writes in English, it is not his native language; he was born Peter Joachim Froehlich in 1923 in Germany, and fled the Nazis 16 years later with his mother and father.

Unlike others thus affected by Nazism, Gay does not see himself as a victim and declines to present himself as such. By contrast with millions of others, he suffered relatively little survival humiliation and injury and made "hundreds" of

when presented to Gay led him to ask: "Why didn't we pack our bags and leave the country the day after Hitler came to power?" This memoir is an attempt to address that question, in personal terms but ones that have broader pertinence.

The beloved only child of middle-class parents — his father was in "the crystal and china business" — who were highly cultured and strongly attached to a large extended family, Gay grew up thinking of himself far less as a Jew than as a German. "There are those ways of becoming a Jew," he writes; "by birth, by conversion, by decree." The Nazis, as they began to crack down on Jews in the early 1930s, made him a member of that group, but he and his parents "did not want to be Jews by Nazi edict, their definition of our 'race' was just another lie that we repudiated as unhistorical and unscientific."

To some extent the Froehlichs, like the Franz-Corman in their famous garden, simply denied what they saw all around them. But two things mattered more. One was that "we were Germans; the gangsters who had taken control of the country were not Germans — we were." The other was that for a long time life seemed pretty much as it always had, a "reminder that major public tremors and mundane private matters easily co-existed." It was harder then than it is in hindsight to work up a sense of urgency, nor did not come until the summer of 1938, when Gay's father was evicted from his firm.

"without compensation and, given the Nazis' legal and judicial system, without recourse."

It was then, as "other portents proliferated and at unprecedented speed," that the little family began to try to flee. It was able to do so because of the courage and persistence of Gay's father, the convenience of having close relatives in Florida and a substantial amount of plain good luck. The Froehlichs missed the gas chambers by little more than a wink and a whistle.

They went first to Havana, then to the United States, where they settled in Colorado. Young Peter set about becoming American with determination — his change of name was an early move in that direction — and soon became an American success. But the "vast political distance from Nazi Germany, even the first act we had yearned so desperately to breathe, had not automatically diminished the pressure of the past, let alone erased it.

It took a long time for Gay to reach an accommodation with Berlin, a city he had loved deeply. He describes his reluctance to cross the border into Germany, his apprehension that as a Jew he would be treated cruelly, his impatience with those who misunderstood the complex situation in which, as a boy, he had lived. He knows even now, that Gay many will always stir deep responses within him, many of them unpleasant, but he has come to terms with it.

Washington Post Service

CHESS

By Robert Byrne

PETROV DEFENSE

YOU hear a lot of complaints from tournament players about what a burden it is keeping abreast of the latest developments in opening practice. New ... the computer has been pressed into service, and its remarkable speed makes it possible to add an enormous number of openings to your and your opponents ... repertoire. In the game between the ...

(chess analysis text, partly illegible)

Position after 28...Bh3

CROSSWORD

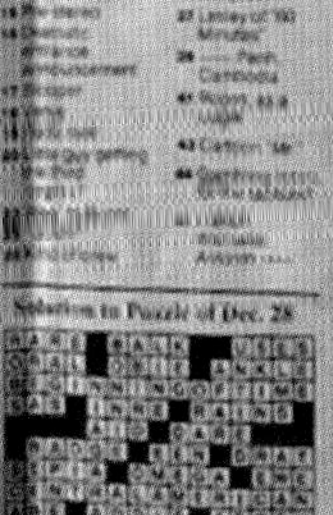

© New York Times/Edited by Will Shortz

N°.07 Living-room conquerors

chairwear \ tablecare \ doorflair (Limited Editions)

FOR INFORMATIONS CALL: PRESS PARIS +33-1-42.01.51.00 • PRESS MILANO +39-02-58.10.55.20 • BLESS PARIS +33-1-48.01.87.43 • BLESS BERLIN +49-30-44.02.46.42
www.bless-service.de (webdesign by Jens Jacob) • showroom in Paris during fashion week

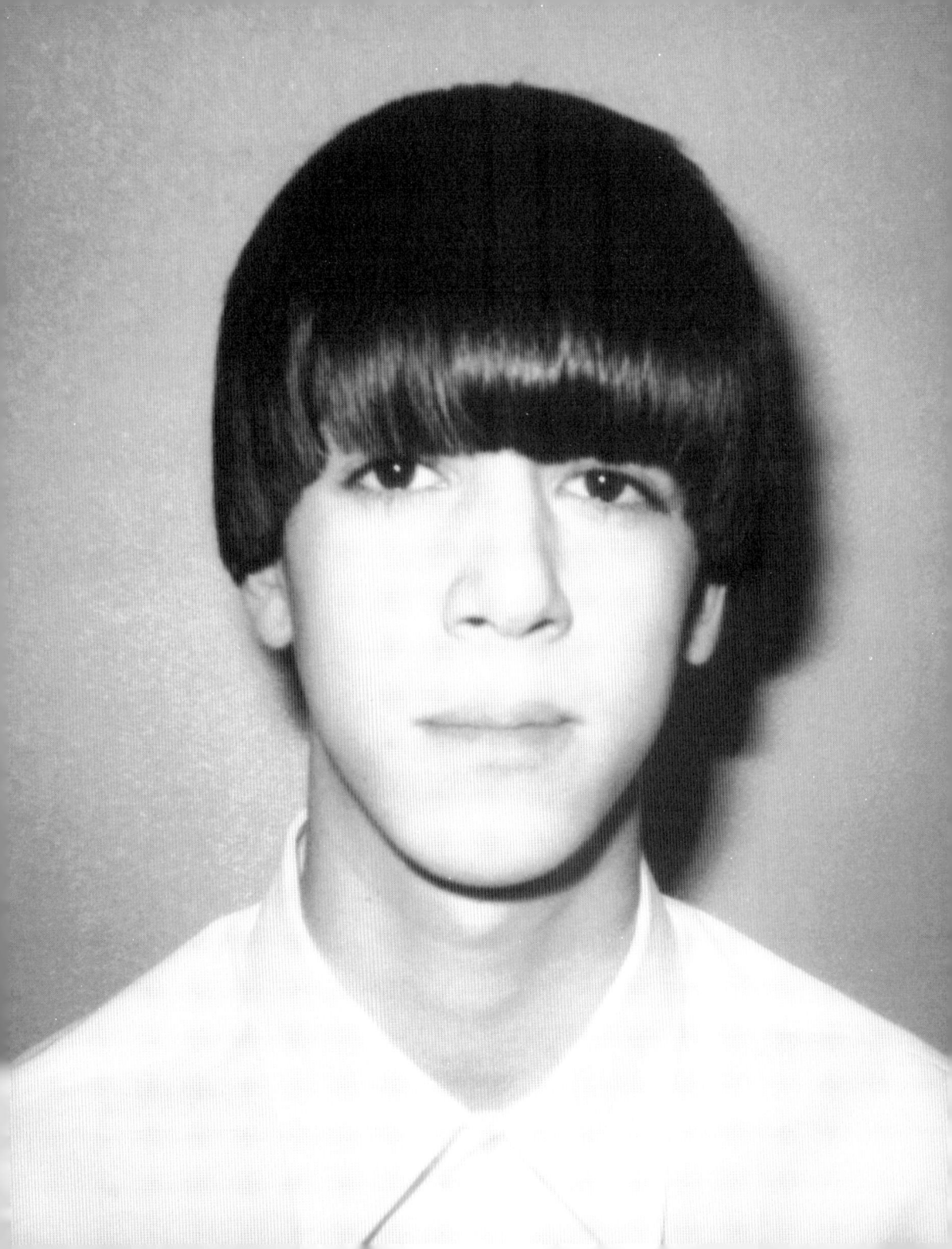

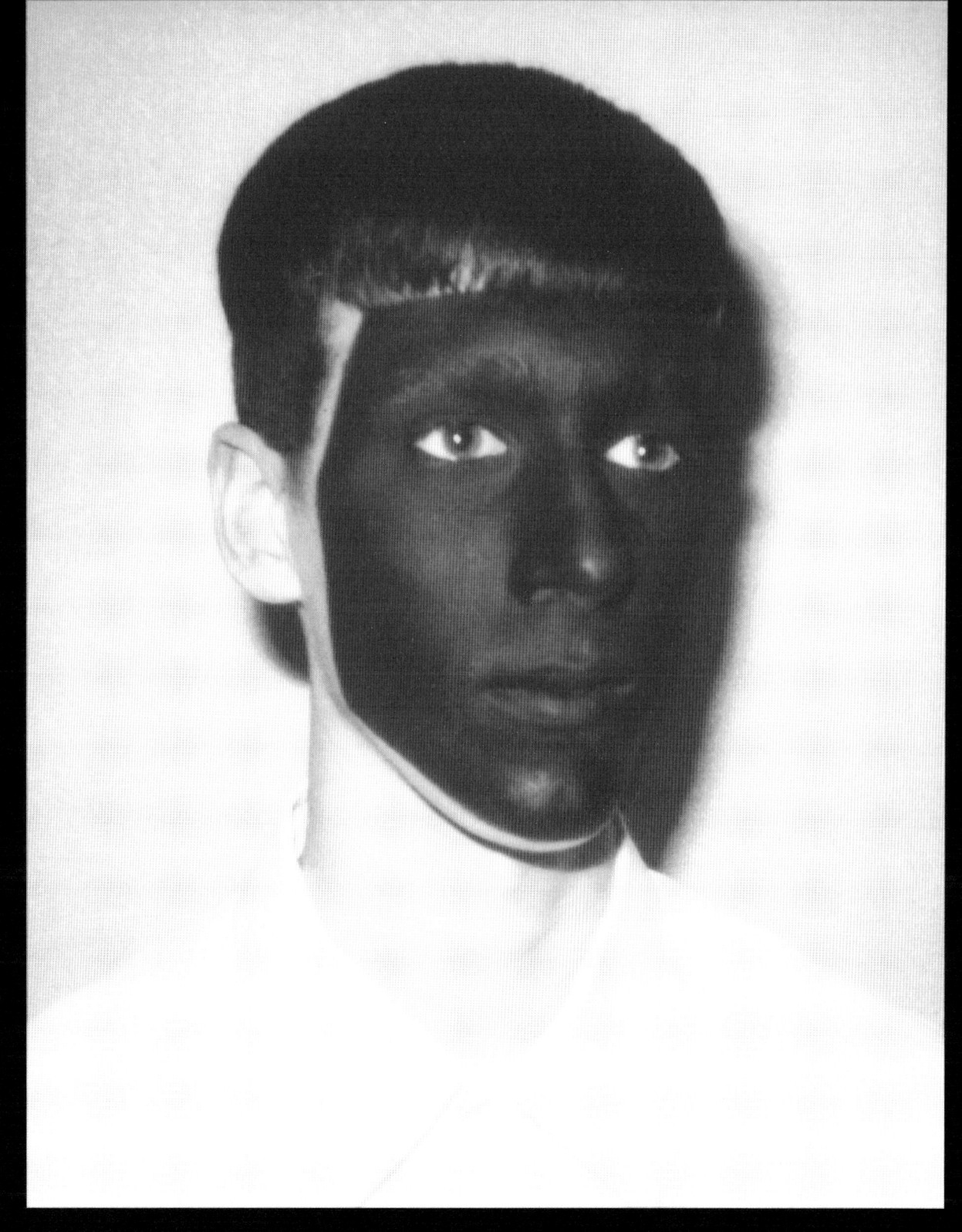

DISORDER

49.23.79.79 FAX 33-1-49.23.79.90   PRESS TOKYO: TAKAO SAKAYORI C/O RAVEN & WOLF TEL 81-3-3406.0668 FAX 81-3-3406.0687   RAF SIMONS OFFICE: VLEMINCKVELD 68 B-2000 ANTWERPEN TEL 32-3-231.54

PHOTOGRAPHY

MARK BORTHWICK FOR PURPLE
ANUSCHKA BLOMMERS AND NIELS SCHUMM FOR SELF SERVICE 9

RESTYLED BY

PASCALE GATZEN AND THOMAS BUXÓ

crazy. Be eclectic. Unconventional. Outrageous. Fall's most madcap designs are a hyper mix of vivid colors, tactile fabrics and unexpected details. With their unfinished edges, nubby weaves, faux-fur trim and organic accessories, these clothes practically vibrate a raw edge of their own. Go with it. Opposite page: Slate-gray silk chiffon ruched minidress, about $3,420, Valentino Boutique. Ebony necklace, Kris Rhus for Yohji Yamamoto. Eye-opener: Estée Lauder Uncircle Eye Treatment. Fashion editor: Melanie Ward. Photographed by David Sims

Helmut Lang?

Audrey in my garden.

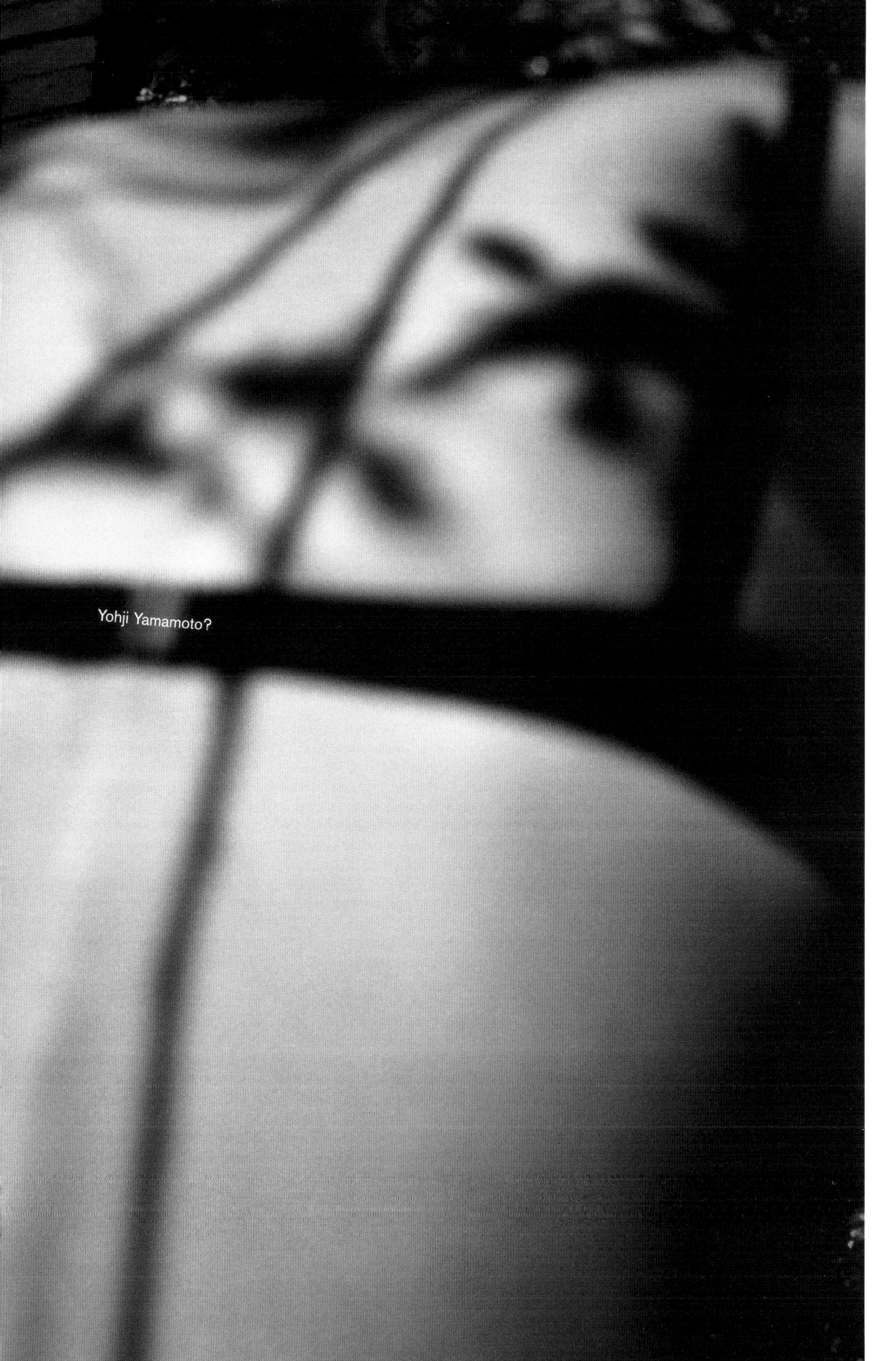
Yohji Yamamoto?

body art

A chic woman has always clenched her **bag** in her fist, hung it from her shoulder or dangled it ladylike from her wrist. This season, she simply straps a cool pack on **her waist**, hip or leg. Now your bag is an extension of yourself—literally. Opposite page: Wool plaid belt bag, Couture Givenchy by Alexander McQueen. To order at Givenchy, NYC. This page: White cotton holster bag, about $155, Helmut Lang. At Louis, Boston, Boston. Fashion editor: Richard Sinnott. Photographed by Richard Burbridge.

THE GG eGG

Marilyn Monroe big knickers from SELFRIDGES

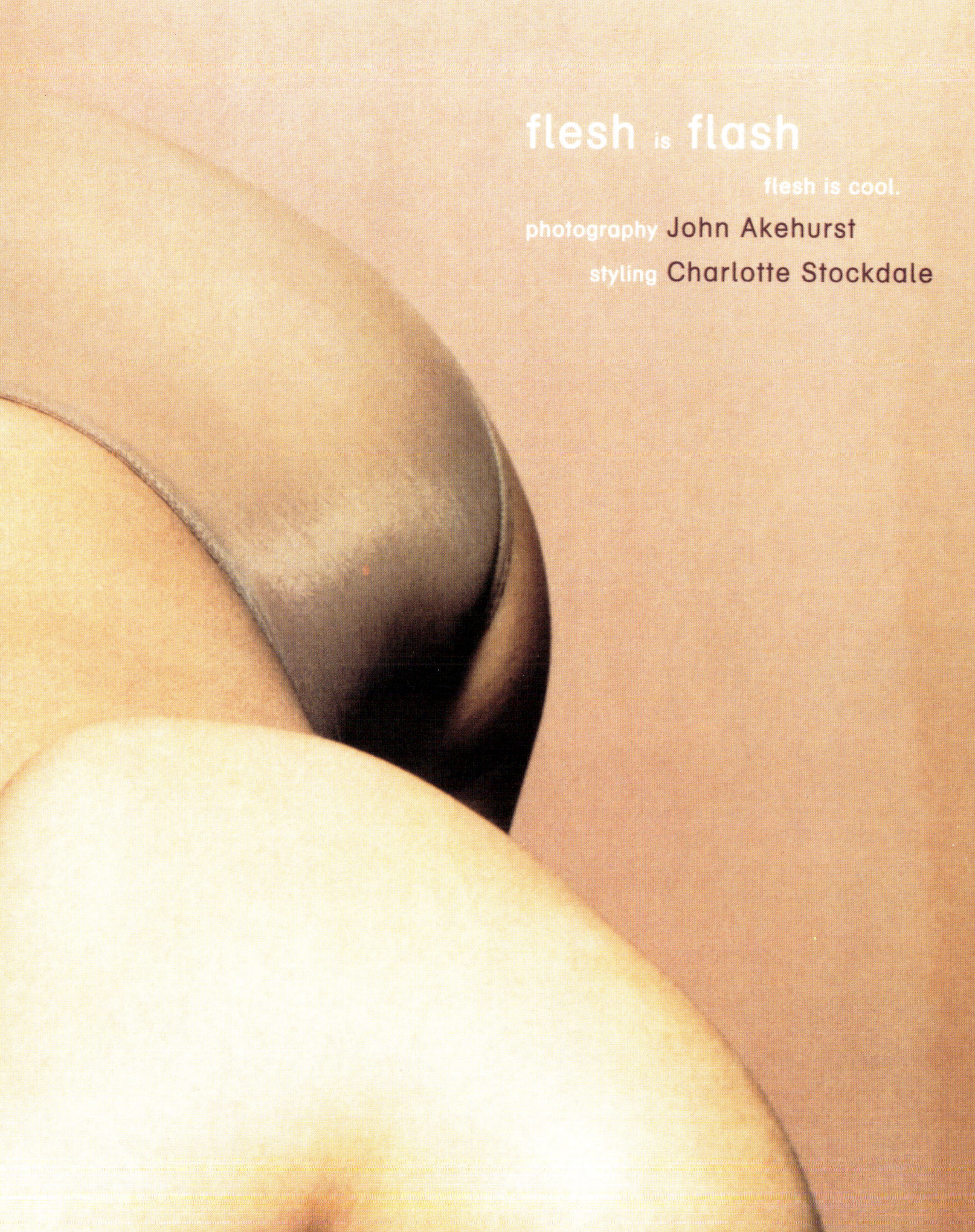

flesh is flash

flesh is cool.

photography John Akehurst

styling Charlotte Stockdale

Iris wears human hair earring by SARAH HARMANEE for ALEXANDER MCQUEEN; feather ring by KATIE CLARKE

Trompe l'oeil tweed—**Karl Lagerfeld**'s evening dress is of loosely woven fluorescent threads on tulle, this page: Multicolored wool-blend tweed dress with patch pockets, about $2870, **Chanel**. At Chanel, NYC. Soft edges: Chanel Lèvres Double Soin Lip Cure. Classic feminine details like eyelets and beading soften up **Valentino**'s leather-and-suede evening dress, opposite page: White long beaded Western dress with suede bodice and leather appliqué skirt, Valentino Boutique. To order at Valentino boutiques, NYC, Los Angeles and Palm Beach, FL.

Sara Daykin. *Age :* 15. *Where do you live ?* Manchester.
Favorite movie ? Titanic. Favorite actor ? Leonardo Di Caprio. *Favorite designer ?* None, but my favorite shop is Top Shop. *Favorite singer or band ? The Verve* because they are exellent. *Are you a fan ?* Of football (Manchester United). *What is fashionable ?* Bootleg trousers. *What isn't fashionable ?* Leggings ! *Why and how do you start modelling ?* I was scouted in Manchester in a shopping center by Sarah. *Last important thing you bought ?* A suitcase on wheels. *What do you like or dislike about your apparence ?* I like my hair and my eyes but I don't like everything else. What magazines do you read and like ? *Elle. Favorite TV show or channel ? Coronation Street.* What job would you like to do later ? Model, holiday rep or physiotherapist. Best and worst thing about being a teen ? Nothing and everything. *Do you have a hobby ?* Talking on the phone and cinema. *How do you see yourself in 10 years ?* I don't think that far ahead !
Sara Daykin wears a black acrylic turtleneck sweater by Véronique Branquinho.

Ruth Papworth. *Age : 15. Where do you live ? Surrey. Favorite movie ? The Craft. Favorite actor ?* Paul Nichols. *Favorite designer ?* Miss Selfridge, I don't have favorite designer. *Favorite singer or band ?* Garbage. *Why ?* There cool, good styling, I like their attitude. *Are you a fan ?* I like watching the world cup. *What is fashionable ?* Combat trousers. *What isn't fashionable ?* The colour pink and podal pushers. *Last important thing you bought ?* A Marylin Manson CD. *What do you like or dislike about your apparence ?* Bad hair. I can live with everything else. *What magazines do you read and like ?* Kerrang, Metal Music magazine. *Favorite TV show or channel ?* Anithing with travel. *What job would you like to do later ?* Anything to do with travel. *Best and worst thing about being a teen ?* School. *Do you have a hobby ?* Going out with friends. *How do you see yourself in 10 years ?* Happy I hope.
Ruth Papworth wears a caramel acrylic turtle neck sweater by Véronique Branquinho.

ALONG A FALSE EQUATOR
MARCH 95
THE REALITY OF THE SENSES
A REPETITIVE PATTERN OF SENSATIONS FELT IN THE WOMB
AND SUSTAINED IN OUR DAILY LIVES THROUGH OUR EXPERIENCES
OF RHYTHM, SPEED AND SOUND . . .
A MEDITATIVE HYPER-SENSORY STATE WHERE THE ARTIFICIAL,
THE NATURAL AND THE TECHNOLOGICAL CONVERGE IN AN ALTERNATIVE FORM.

by mikael jansson

White nylon jacket and white nylon pants **Prada Sport**

CH 72

Sportmax

Joop!

PER LEI: MICROABITO DI
PELLE METALLIZZATA; PER
LUI: CAMICIA DI COTONE E
PANTALONI TUTTO ICEBERG.
STIVALI ARGENTO, HERMÈS.

#58 Oliver in Dolce & Gabbana

#59 Maggie in Clinique

#89 Seijo and Carly in the Jeep wearing Missoni

Acid yellow silk tank top and fuchsia pink silk skirt with ruffles Matthew Williamson

air and makeup Fiona Thomas
odels Ina and Brian

some nerve

In fashion as in art, what shocks initially can come to look classic. But what's shocking anymore? **Katherine Betts** looks at the avant-garde today, and **Steven Meisel** pays tribute to some artistic innovators.

Sisters of protest: Inspired by a performance piece by Leslie Labowitz and Suzanne Lacy, a trio of fashion rebels causes a stir in Hussein Chalayan's wool hood capes. Details, stores, see In This Issue.
Fashion Editor: Camilla Nickerson

Horse hair coat and patent leather mules
by **Givenchy Haute couture**
created by Alexander McQueen

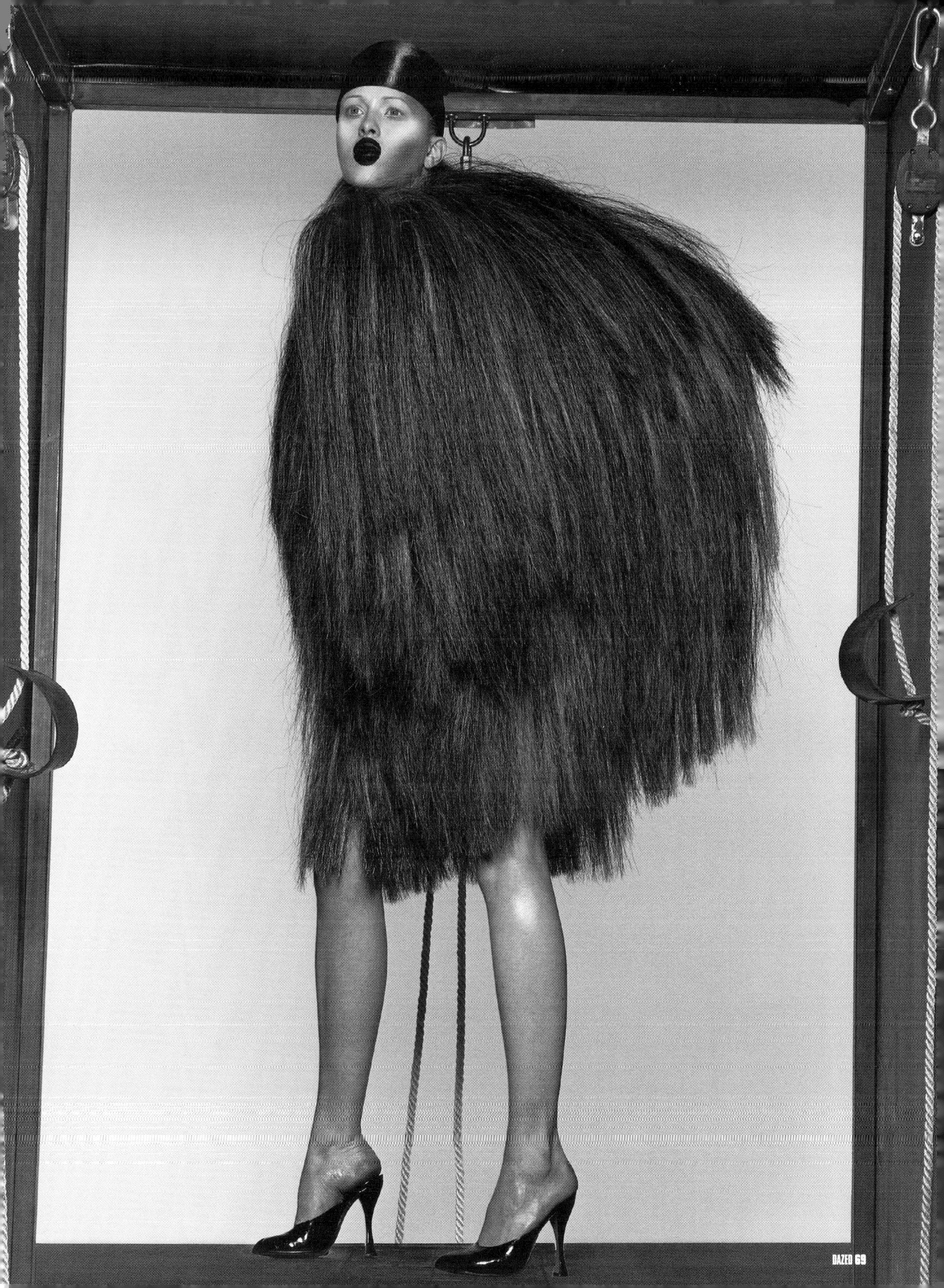

When you need a little excitement, an aqua
top adds voltage to a gray shift, opposite page:
Charcoal stretch wool dress, about $600, aqua
stretch nylon jersey top (worn underneath), about
$670. Both, Richard Tyler Collection. At Ultimo,
Chicago and Dallas. Night shift: Estée Lauder
100% Time Release Moisture Creme. Under the
suburban skies—take the chill out of the evening
air by slipping on a classic, simple balmacaan,
this page: Pale-blue wool coat, about $1565,
Marc Jacobs. At Bloomingdale's, NYC.

SILVER

SEXY FOIL-LIKE DRESSES, SHINY SANDALS, METALLIC MAKE-UP AND EVEN A LITTLE SHINE FOR THE HOME. THEY MIGHT BE WORTH THEIR WEIGHT IN GOLD, BUT THEY'RE MUCH MORE FIERCE IN SILVER. THIS PAGE: POP MIRROR, ABOUT $1600, ROBERT MING. OPPOSITE PAGE: BLACK DRESS WITH SILVER MYLAR APPLIQUÉS AND LACE-UP COLLAR, ABOUT $2500, AND SOCKS AND HIGH-TOPS. ALL, ISSEY MIYAKE. DRESS AT ISSEY MIYAKE, NYC. GALAXY-GIRL SCENT: ISSEY MIYAKE L'EAU D'ISSEY EAU DE TOILETTE. FASHION EDITOR: MELANIE WARD. PHOTOGRAPHED BY RAYMOND MEIER

SURVIVAL OF THE FITTEST
THIS PAGE: An olive toggle jacket (about $185) and orange pants (about $220) for the urban warrior. All by Maharishi. Alan Bilzerian, Boston. OPPOSITE PAGE: This street soldier sports details from motorcycle racing (padded knees) and fencing (flawless white). Print tank, about $90, sheer tank, about $335, and cotton pants, about $270, all by Helmut Lang. Helmut Lang Boutique, NYC. Details, more stores; see In This Issue.

Wrapping yourself in a thick, toasty sweater and a soft quilted skirt is one chic way to feel warm and cozy. Opposite page, left: Cream cashmere sweater, about $425, Isaac Mizrahi. At select Saks Fifth Avenue stores. Quilted wool skirt, about $1470, Guglielmo Capone. At Weathervane, Santa Monica. Right: Black wool cable-knit turtleneck, about $560, skirt and leather sandals. All, Guglielmo Capone. At Weathervane, Santa Monica. This page: Black mohair mock turtleneck top, about $210, Atsuro Tayama. At Atsuro Tayama, NYC. Staying power: Bain de Terre Beezwax Styling Stick.

Da sinistra. Abito lungo di
lana dévorée e organza
blu con stola di finto pelo.
Due abiti di garza di lana
e organza beige con
ricami oro su shorts in
colore contrasto. Tutto
Comme des Garçons.

YVES SAINT LAURENT'S
SNOW-WHITE FULL-LENGTH
MINK AND ITS SATIN GOWN
BRING BACK THAT VINTAGE
HOLLYWOOD GLAMOUR.
Opposite page: White mink coat,
Yves Saint Laurent Fourrures. Ivory
satin (Schlaepfer) long evening gown,
Yves Saint Laurent Haute Couture.
Both made to order at Yves Saint
Laurent Haute Couture, Paris. Belt,
Yves Saint Laurent. Local color: Yves
Saint Laurent Paris parfum.

SWEEPING STATEMENT.
JOHN GALLIANO'S BILLOWY
FUR-TRIMMED COAT FOR
CHRISTIAN DIOR EXEMPLIFIES
HIS FLAIR FOR THEATRICS.
This page: White silk taffeta (Bucol)
coat with fox shawl collar, Christian
Dior Haute Couture by John Galliano.
Made to order at Christian Dior
Haute Couture, Paris. Ultrafeminine:
Christian Dior Dionissimo parfum. This
portfolio: Hair, Orlando Pita; makeup,
Diane Kendal for Aveda.

Maiden Voyage

It's an age-old story, even in China: Young country girl moves to the big city, where she finds a career, love, happiness—and the newest fashions.

PHOTOGRAPHED BY CARTER SMITH

CONSTRUCTIVISMES

КНИГИ

КНИГИ

ПО ВСЕ
ОТРАСЛ
ЗНАНИ

Il aura fallu attendre la perestroïka pour considérer le constructivisme comme un mouvement artistique essentiel du XXᵉ siècle plutôt qu'un objet de propagande communiste. Refus d'un esthétisme futile au profit d'œuvres raisonnées, utiles à la collectivité ; volonté de confondre art et art appliqué : aujourd'hui, cette révolution-là dure encore. Et l'œuvre d'un Malevitch, savants calculs de géométrie et de couleurs, comme celle d'un Rodchenko, qui n'en finit pas de réinventer l'espace, restent d'une formidable actualité. **Photos Michael Thompson.**

HOMMAGE À RODCHENKO
PAGE DE GAUCHE, INTERPRÉTATION DE SON «AFFICHE POUR LIVRES», 1924. ROBE
COURTE ZIPPÉE EN CRÊPE DE LAINE MARINE, À GALON ET POIGNETS REBRODÉS DE
PASTILLES EN SOIE COLORÉES, ET PETIT FICHU ASSORTI, **CHANEL**.
CI-DESSUS, PULL EN MAILLE DE LAINE BEIGE À COL MARRON, **BALENCIAGA**. COIFFURE
SERGE NORMANT. MISE EN BEAUTÉ SCOTT ANDREW. RÉALISATION DELPHINE TREANTON.

"Nous n'avons pas besoin d'un mausolée de l'art où adorer les œuvres mortes, mais d'usines vivantes de l'esprit humain – dans les rues, dans les tramways, dans les usines, les ateliers et les habitations des travailleurs."
Maïakovski

HOOVEY GiRl

photography <u>Steven Klein</u>
styling <u>Nancy Rohde</u>

In the land of the
giants, the
futuristic peasant
wench is king

Brown crushed cotton dress by Jil Sander; cream
wool tights worn as gloves by Wolford; twisted
muslin around neck from Wolfin Textiles

A simple A-line or pleated skirt seems collegiate, but worn with heels and the right flair it's sexy and womanly. Opposite page, left: cashmere turtleneck, about $700, and tweed wool skirt, about $400. Both, Bottega Veneta. At Bottega Veneta, NYC and Beverly Hills. Stilettos, Manolo Blahnik. Right: Shirt and jumper, GapKids. This page: Navy wool peacoat, about $475, white shirt, about $190, and gray knife-pleated skirt, about $300. All, Nicole Farhi. At select Saks Fifth Avenue stores. Pumps, Manolo Blahnik. Handbag, Gucci.

Helmut Lang's gray wool skirt, at
Helmut Lang, New York. **Chanel**'s gray
cotton shirt, by Karl Lagerfeld.
Wolford hosiery; Bottega Veneta shoes.

Yohji Yamamoto's cotton top and
embroidered silk skirt, at Linda
Dresner, Detroit; Susan, Burlingame,
California; Yohji Yamamoto, New York.
Yohji Yamamoto hat and gloves.

Left: Wool cardigan with fur collar by Kosuke Tsumura; felt dress by Shelley Fox; silver ear lobe clip by Naomi Filmer
Right: Top and skirt, both by Helmut Lang; silver finger piece by Alexander McQueen

I'm not exactly in condition for slinky slipdresses.
Photography by Anuschka Blommers and Niels Schumm
Styling by Suzanne Koller
Assisted by Christopher Niquet
🎧 Music by Frédéric Sanchez :
Pj Harvey *"The Wind"*&*"The Garden"*, Sonic Youth *"Anagrama"*

What could be easier than throwing on a jersey dress? Opposite page: Black rayon jersey tube skirt (worn as a dress), about $130, Adrienne Vittadini; white bandeau, about $28, Nancy Ganz Bodyslimmers. Snake-chain belt, Tony Graham; sandals, Manolo Blahnik for Michael Kors. Sleek, glossy, and straight: Redken Smooth Anti-Frizz Creme. This page: Chocolate matte jersey halterdress, about $875, Celine.

BLACK LEATHER KIMONO COAT CUSTOMISED WITH LEATHER STRINGS :
KOSTAS MURKUDIS

White short sleeve cotton shirt by **Justin Oh**; white pleated tennis skirt by **Polo Ralph Lauren**; original Levis denim stetson hat from portobello market

uneasy

Photography by Anushka Blommers
Styling by Suzanne Koller
Assisted by Christopher Niquet
Hair by Marion Anee @ On air. Make-up by Ingrid Boekel @ House of Orange
Model : Ciara @ Select.

♫ Music by Frederic Sanchez :
Hovercraft *"Vagus Nerva"* Remixed by Scanner
and *"D-Orbit Burn"* Remixed by Scanner (IRE)

White paper dress by Junya Watanabe.
Ballerina shoes by Repetto.

Get tanked: Tank tops are warm-weather staples. **Far left:** Leather jacket, $1,350, leather skirt with mirror trim, $1,060; both, Prada. **Left:** Ribbon-knit tank, $530, embroidered silk skirt, $2,850; both, Narciso Rodriguez. For details, see Shopping Guide.
■ **BEAUTYWATCH** Physicians Formula Sun Shield self-tanner combines the best of both worlds: tan skin and SPF 20 protection.

Trussardi's black nylon and Lycra
spandex turtleneck, at Henri Bendel,
New York; La Dolce, Austin, Texas.

Ann Demeulemeester's black wool and
polyamide coat, at Alan Bilzerian, Boston;
Bagutta, New York; Barneys, New York.

Prada's black silk dress with plastic
film strip appliques, by Miuccia Prada, at
Barneys, New York; Prada, New York.

[this page]
Donna Karan's black silk organza dress and silk coat, at select Nordstrom and Bloomingdale's stores. Fred Leighton earrings and brooch; Ralph Lauren socks.

[opposite]
Stained glass window in the Cathedral of Ayacucho.

This feature styled by Alexandra White. Hair by Mark Lopez; makeup by Tom Pecheux for Kiehl's; models: Angela Lindval/IMG and Freddy Eliot. Fashion Assistant: Jennifer Hitzges. Arrangements made by Prom Perú. Production assistant: Nino Penaloza. Photographed in Peru, where the crew stayed at Hotel El Olivar de San Isidro in Lima and the Ayacucho Hotel Plaza in Ayacucho. For more details, see Personal Shopper, page 174.

White Noise

White has never been so screaming. These pieces shout out in strong, moveable, sexy shapes—short shifts, long flowing dresses, daring necks, and serious pants. Pretty aggressive for a noncolor, no? Opposite page: Cotton jersey short-sleeved long dress with inner ties around neck, about $290, Ann Demeulemeester. Greek sandals, Jimmy Choo. Spring into action: Body Shine in Pink Shimmer by Chanel and In the Buff body gloss by Philosophy. Fashion editor: Melanie Ward. Photographed by Craig McDean

CARREFOUR, ONE OF THE BIGGEST SUPERMARKET CHAINS FOUND OUTSIDE PARIS OR ANY OTHER FRENCH CITY, IS THE LARGEST PRODUCER AND DISTRIBUTOR OF CLOTHES IN FRANCE.

Silk-chiffon lattice-print dress by Gianni Versace.
Fishnet tights by Jonathan Aston

This page: vintage print
dress by YVES ST LAURENT;
leather wraparound belt by
OTTO GLANZ; black tights
around head by FOGAL

Opposite: vintage white shirt
by TED LAPIDUS; Afghan coin
necklace from RAU; black
tights around head by FOGAL

photography
Inez Van Lamsweerde
& Vinoodh Matadin

doll

drums

C'mon Gertie, let's go party!

styling Nancy Rohde

Multi-layered
pleated print dress
by COMME DES
GARÇONS; suede
fringe Pocahontas
boots from
WESTERN SPIRIT;
black tights around
head by FOGAL

PHIL : CLEAR GREY PANTS, BLUE COTON SHIRT, BLACK
SCHOOLBOY TIE, BLACK REVERSIBLE CORDUROY VELVET
JACKET, BLACK CONVERSE. NICK : SLEEVELESS NAVY BLUE
HIGH SCHOOL SWEATER, CLEAR GREY JOGGING SHORTS,
NAVY BLUE COAT, SPORT SOCKS, BLACK CONVERSE.
ALL CLOTHES BY RAF SIMONS.

Springscapes

Take a look at spring's new personalities. Never before have designers shown such diversity in one season. Bazaar chooses very different looks from 19 of the most distinctive designers and shoots them with vintage Hollywood backdrops. Look closely and soon you will see yourself in one of these roles. Start envisioning. Yohji Yamamoto's millennium muse pares down with body-hugging tubes and opera gloves, opposite page: Black silk tube with brown polka dots, about $430, and linen skirt, about $460. Both, and handbag and gloves, Yohji Yamamoto. At Yohji Yamamoto, NYC. Fashion editor: Melanie Ward. Photographed by Craig McDean

incredibly

Photography by Jonathan de Villiers
Styling by Suzanne Koller
Hair by Leslie McMenamin@Untitled using Aveda
Make up by Kate Lee@Untitled using shu emura
Models : Ruth Papworth and Amy Fenton@Select
Styling assistance by Christopher Niquet
Photographic assistance by Paul Burroughs and Kumy Saito
Shot at St John's Westminster-flat for sale and rent via FPDSavills 0171 630 8866
Ω Music by Frederic Sanchez :
Takano Minekawa *"Milk rock", "Cat house"*
Nuno Canavarro *"Alsee", "Cave"*

Ruth wears a square cotton black hand knitted top,
black three-quarter lenght wool pants and
brown high-heeled leather boots all by Nicolas Ghesquière for Balenciaga.

Istante's silk shirt and wool skirt, by Gianni Versace, at Versace boutiques. Kleinberg-Sherrill belt. His wool suit by **Calvin Klein**, at select Marshal Field's stores; **Valentino**'s cotton shirt, at Saks Fifth Avenue, New York.

Donna Karan's double-faced wool dress, at Bergdorf Goodman; Saks Fifth Avenue; Bloomingdale's. Bulgari watch; Petra shoes.

Gottex's nylon and Lycra spandex swimsuit. Monet necklace.
In this feature: Hair by John Sahag; makeup by Dick Page; manicure by Joyce Green for Cloutier; models: Erin O'Connor/Ford; Kristin McMenamy/Next; casting by Terry Berland. Styled by Michel Botbol. Fashion Assistant: Matthew Edelstein.

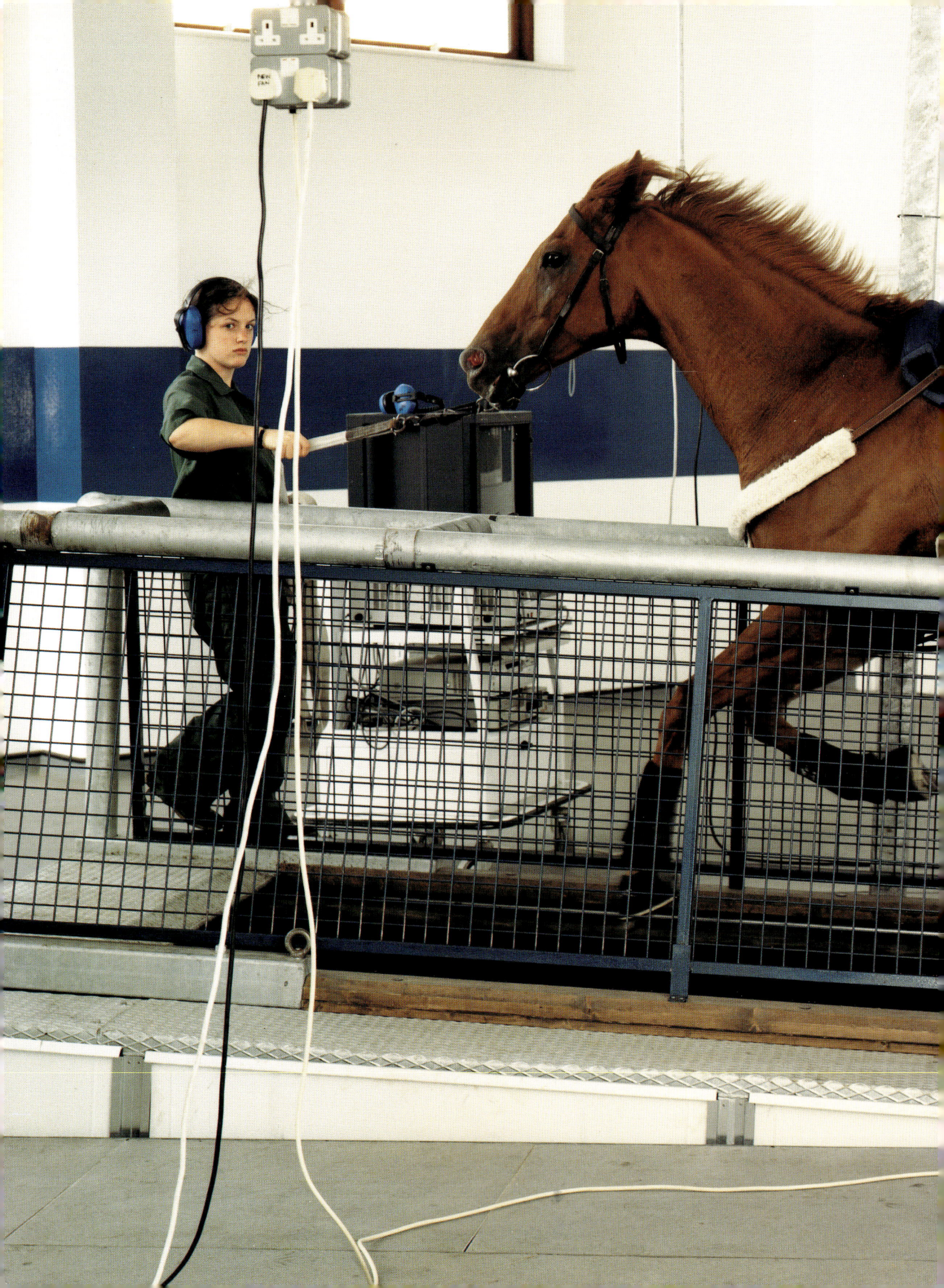

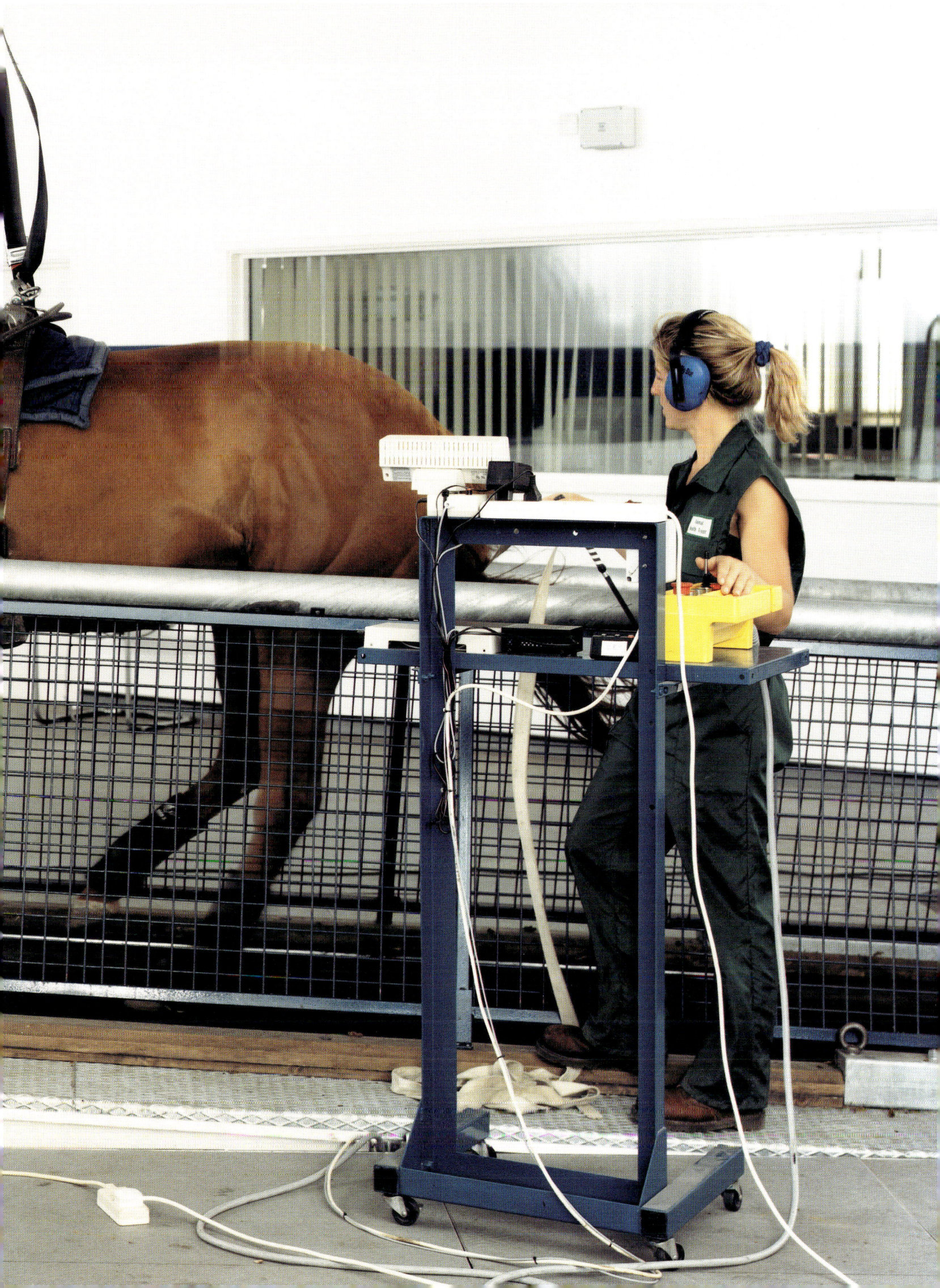

EXCEPTION
AL FASHION
PRESENTAT
ION DESERV
ES EXCEPTI
ONAL PAPER
SIGNATURE® FROM MEAD COATED PAPERS
THE NUMBER ONE CHOICE TO REPRODUCE YOUR SIGNATURE COLLECTION
FASHION PUBLICATION IS PRINTED ON SIGNATURE® GLOSS FROM MEAD COATED PAPERS

Mead

PRINT
INTERNATIONAL